Beyoncé Quiz

101 Questions To Test Your ᴋɴᴏ
Of This Incredibly Successful Musician

By Colin Carter

Beyoncé Quiz

This book contains one hundred and one informative and entertaining trivia questions with multiple choice answers. With 101 questions, some easy, some more demanding, this entertaining book will really test your knowledge of Beyoncé.

You will be quizzed on a wide range of topics associated with Beyoncé for you to test yourself; with questions on her early days, songs, lyrics, achievements, awards and much more, guaranteeing you a truly fun, educational experience.

This quiz book will provide entertainment for fans of all ages and will certainly test your knowledge of this world-famous musician. The book is packed with information and is a must-have for all true Beyoncé fans, wherever you live in the world.

Published by Glowworm Press
glowwormpress.com

ACKNOWLEDGEMENTS

My friend's daughter Alice simply adores Beyoncé.

As a writer, I thought I would write a book on Beyoncé for her to test herself and to see how much she really knows about the legend that is Beyoncé.

She told me that she was not alone, and that Beyoncé had millions of fans and that I should write the book for every one of them, not just her.

So I did!   This book is for all you wonderful Beyoncé fans – wherever you live in the world.

I do hope you enjoy it.

Colin Carter

OK, let's get started with the first set of questions.

Q1. When was Beyoncé born?
  A. 1979
  B. 1980
  C. 1981
  D. 1982

Q2. What star sign is Beyoncé?
  A. Aries
  B. Libra
  C. Sagittarius
  D. Virgo

Q3. Where was Beyoncé born?
  A. Atlanta
  B. Dallas
  C. Houston
  D. New Orleans

Q4. What is Beyoncé's middle name?
  A. Giselle
  B. Michelle
  C. Nicole
  D. Renee

Q5. What is Beyoncé's surname?
  A. Knowing
  B. Knowledge
  C. Knowles

D. Knowlsey

Q6. How many siblings does Beyoncé have?
   A. One
   B. Two
   C. Three
   D. Four

Q7. What is the name of Beyoncé's husband?
   A. Drake
   B. Jay-Z
   C. Kanye West
   D. Pharrell Williams

Q8. Where did Beyoncé meet her husband?
   A. At a concert
   B. At a mutual friend's party
   C. In a recording studio
   D. On a movie set

Q9. When did they marry?
   A. 2006
   B. 2007
   C. 2008
   D. 2009

Q10. What is the name of Beyoncé's first child?
   A. Blue Ivy
   B. North West
   C. Rumi Carter

D. Sir Carter

Here are the answers to the first set of questions.

A1. Beyoncé was born on September 4, 1981. She celebrated her 40th birthday in 2021 with a glamorous party attended by friends and family.

A2. Beyoncé's star sign is Virgo. Virgos are known for their meticulous attention to detail and strong sense of duty.

A3. Beyoncé was born in Houston, Texas. She often references her Texan roots in her music and public appearances.

A4. Beyoncé's middle name is Giselle. This name is of French origin, reflecting her Creole heritage.

A5. Beyoncé's surname is Knowles.

A6. Beyoncé has one sibling, a younger sister named Solange. She is also a successful singer and songwriter.

A7. Beyoncé's husband is Jay-Z, whose real name is Shawn Carter. Jay-Z is a renowned rapper, producer, and entrepreneur.

A8. Beyoncé met Jay-Z in a recording studio. This encounter led to several musical collaborations, which blossomed into a romantic relationship.

A9. Beyoncé and Jay-Z married on April 4, 2008. They had a private ceremony in New York City.

A10. Beyoncé's first child is named Blue Ivy Carter. She was born on January 7, 2012, and has already made appearances in her parents' music videos.

Here is the next set of questions.

Q11. Where did Beyoncé grow up?
 A. Atlanta
 B. Dallas
 C. Houston
 D. New Orleans

Q12. What was Beyoncé's first job?
 A. Backup dancer
 B. Choir singer
 C. Hair salon assistant
 D. Retail clerk

Q13. Which musical instrument did Beyoncé first learn to play?
 A. Drums
 B. Guitar
 C. Piano
 D. Violin

Q14. What color eyes does Beyoncé have?
 A. Blue
 B. Brown
 C. Green
 D. Hazel

Q15. How tall is Beyoncé?
 A. 5'3"
 B. 5'5"

C. 5'7"
D. 5'9"

Q16. What is Beyoncé's nickname?
  A. Bee
  B. Queen B
  C. Sasha Fierce
  D. Yoncé

Q17. What was Beyoncé's first tattoo?
  A. Angel wings
  B. Roman numeral IV
  C. Star
  D. Tree

Q18. What languages does Beyoncé speak?
  A. English and French
  B. English and Spanish
  C. English and Italian
  D. English and Portuguese

Q19. What is the name of Beyoncé's second child?
  A. Blue Carter
  B. North Carter
  C. Rumi Carter
  D. Sir Carter

Q20. What charity work is Beyoncé known for?
  A. Education initiatives
  B. Environmental conservation

C. Hunger relief
D. Women's rights

Here is the latest block of answers.

A11. Beyoncé grew up in Houston, Texas. She started singing and dancing at a young age, performing in local talent shows.

A12. Beyoncé's first job was singing in the church choir. This early experience helped her develop her powerful voice and stage presence.

A13. Beyoncé first learned to play the piano. She often uses her piano skills when composing music.

A14. Beyoncé has brown eyes. Her expressive eyes are often highlighted in her music videos and photo shoots.

A15. Beyoncé is 5'7" tall. Her height, combined with her stage presence, makes her a commanding performer.

A16. Beyoncé's nickname is "Queen B." This nickname reflects her status as a leading figure in the music industry.

A17. Beyoncé's first tattoo was a Roman numeral IV. The number four is significant to her, representing her birth date, her wedding date, and other important milestones.

A18. Beyoncé speaks English and some Spanish. She has performed songs in Spanish and has expressed an interest in learning more languages.

A19. Beyoncé's second child is named Rumi Carter. Rumi is one of the twins born to Beyoncé and Jay-Z on June 13, 2017.

A20. Beyoncé is known for her work in women's rights. She has supported numerous initiatives that empower women and girls around the world.

Let's move on to some questions about her career.

Q21. What was the name of the first record label Beyoncé signed to?
    A. Atlantic Records
    B. Columbia Records
    C. Def Jam Recordings
    D. Roc Nation

Q22. What is the name of Beyoncé's first album?
    A. B'Day
    B. Dangerously in Love
    C. I Am... Sasha Fierce
    D. Lemonade

Q23. When was this debut album released?
    A. 2001
    B. 2003
    C. 2005
    D. 2007

Q24. What was the first single Beyoncé ever released?
    A. Baby Boy
    B. Crazy in Love
    C. Déjà Vu
    D. Irreplaceable

Q25. What is the name of Beyoncé's second album?
    A. 4

B. B'Day
C. Dangerously in Love
D. I Am... Sasha Fierce

Q26. What is the name of Beyoncé's third album?
  A. 4
  B. B'Day
  C. Dangerously in Love
  D. I Am... Sasha Fierce

Q27. When did Beyoncé first reach the top of the US singles chart?
  A. 2000
  B. 2003
  C. 2006
  D. 2008

Q28. Which was Beyoncé's first number one album in the US?
  A. 4
  B. B'Day
  C. Dangerously in Love
  D. I Am... Sasha Fierce

Q29. What is Beyoncé's vocal range classified as?
  A. Alto
  B. Contralto
  C. Mezzo-soprano
  D. Soprano

Q30. What was the first musical instrument Beyoncé learnt to play?
  A. Drums
  B. Guitar
  C. Piano
  D. Violin

Here are the answers to the last block of questions.

A21. Beyoncé first signed with Columbia Records. This partnership helped launch her career with Destiny's Child and later as a solo artist.

A22. Beyoncé's first album is "Dangerously in Love." It included hit singles such as "Crazy in Love" and "Baby Boy."

A23. Beyoncé's debut album "Dangerously in Love" was released on June 24, 2003. The album received widespread critical acclaim and solidified her status as a solo artist.

A24. The first single Beyoncé ever released was "Crazy in Love." Featuring Jay-Z, the song became a massive hit and is considered one of her signature tracks.

A25. Beyoncé's second album is "B'Day." Released in 2006, it includes hits like "Déjà Vu" and "Irreplaceable."

A26. Beyoncé's third album is "I Am... Sasha Fierce." Released in 2008, the album features the hit singles "Single Ladies (Put a Ring on It)" and "Halo."

A27. Beyoncé first reached the top of the US singles chart in 2003 with "Crazy in Love." The single dominated the Billboard Hot 100 for eight consecutive weeks.

A28. Beyoncé's first number one album in the US was "Dangerously in Love." It debuted at number one on the Billboard 200 chart in 2003.

A29. Beyoncé's vocal range is classified as mezzo-soprano. Her voice spans approximately three octaves, showcasing her versatility and power.

A30. Beyoncé first learned to play the piano. She often uses her piano skills when composing music and during her performances.

Let's have some music video related questions.

Q31. Where was the music video for "Drunk in Love" filmed?
    A. California
    B. Hawaii
    C. New York
    D. Texas

Q32. What music video features Beyoncé dressed as a beauty queen?
    A. Crazy in Love
    B. Pretty Hurts
    C. Run the World (Girls)
    D. Single Ladies (Put a Ring on It)

Q33. Which music video includes Beyoncé riding a horse?
    A. Formation
    B. Halo
    C. Irreplaceable
    D. Sweet Dreams

Q34. Where was the music video for "XO" filmed?
    A. Amusement park
    B. Beach
    C. Desert
    D. Forest

Q35. Which music video features Beyoncé dancing in a flooded mansion?
    A. Haunted
    B. Partition
    C. Sorry
    D. Yoncé

Q36. What music video showcases Beyoncé leading an army of women?
    A. Crazy in Love
    B. Diva
    C. Run the World (Girls)
    D. Upgrade U

Q37. Where was the music video for "Baby Boy" filmed?
    A. Bahamas
    B. Jamaica
    C. Miami
    D. Puerto Rico

Q38. What music video features Beyoncé as a secret agent?
    A. Check on It
    B. Naughty Girl
    C. Partition
    D. Telephone

Q39. Who directed the music video for "Crazy in Love"?

A. David Fincher
B. Francis Lawrence
C. Jake Nava
D. Mark Romanek

Q40. Which music video features Beyoncé performing a dance routine in a white leotard?
A. Déjà Vu
B. Naughty Girl
C. Single Ladies (Put a Ring on It)
D. Sweet Dreams

Here are the answers to the music video questions.

A31. The music video for "Drunk in Love" was filmed on a beach in California. The video features a raw and intimate portrayal of Beyoncé and Jay-Z.

A32. The music video for "Pretty Hurts" features Beyoncé as a beauty queen. The video critiques societal standards of beauty and the pressures women face to conform to these ideals.

A33. The music video for "Formation" includes scenes of Beyoncé riding a horse. The video addresses various themes, including police brutality, black culture, and Southern heritage.

A34. The music video for "XO" was filmed at an amusement park, specifically Coney Island in New York. The video captures a carefree and joyful atmosphere.

A35. The music video for "Haunted" features Beyoncé dancing in a flooded mansion. The eerie and stylish video complements the song's haunting vibe.

A36. The music video for "Run the World (Girls)" showcases Beyoncé leading an army of women. The video is a powerful anthem celebrating female empowerment and strength.

A37. The music video for "Baby Boy" was filmed in Miami. The tropical setting and vibrant visuals enhance the song's Caribbean-inspired sound.

A38. The music video for "Telephone," a collaboration with Lady Gaga, features Beyoncé as a secret agent. The video is a continuation of the storyline from Lady Gaga's "Paparazzi" video.

A39. The music video for "Crazy in Love" was directed by Jake Nava. The video's dynamic energy and chemistry between Beyoncé and Jay-Z helped it become one of her most iconic works.

A40. The music video for "Single Ladies (Put a Ring on It)" features Beyoncé performing a dance routine in a white leotard. The choreography, created by JaQuel Knight, became a global dance phenomenon.

Let's have some lyrics related questions.

Q41. Which song starts with the lyrics, "Remember those walls I built, well baby they're tumbling down"?
   A. Crazy in Love
   B. Halo
   C. Irreplaceable
   D. Single Ladies (Put a Ring on It)

Q42. Which song starts with the lyrics, "You're everything I thought you never were, and nothing like I thought you could've been"?
   A. Crazy in Love
   B. Irreplaceable
   C. Me, Myself and I
   D. Resentment

Q43. Which song starts with the lyrics, "I love your face, you love the taste"?
   A. Dance for You
   B. Partition
   C. Rocket
   D. XO

Q44. Which song starts with the lyrics, "I thought that things like this get better with time"?
   A. Broken-Hearted Girl
   B. Irreplaceable
   C. Love on Top

D. Sorry

Q45. Which song starts with the lyrics, "Ten Hail Marys, I meditate for practice"?
A. 6 Inch
B. Formation
C. Sorry
D. Yoncé

Q46. Which song starts with the lyrics, "I been on, I been on, I been on"?
A. Flawless
B. Freedom
C. Haunted
D. Partition

Q47. Which song starts with the lyrics, "Baby I see you working hard, I want to let you know I'm proud"?
A. Crazy in Love
B. Dance for You
C. Naughty Girl
D. Upgrade U

Q48. Which song starts with the lyrics, "I've been waking up drenched in sweat"?
A. 6 Inch
B. Daddy Lessons
C. Sandcastles
D. Sorry

Q49. Which song starts with the lyrics, "I tried to change, closed my mouth more"?
   A. Don't Hurt Yourself
   B. Freedom
   C. Love Drought
   D. Sandcastles

Q50. Which song starts with the lyrics, "I remember being young, so brave I knew what I needed"?
   A. All Night
   B. Freedom
   C. Formation
   D. Pray You Catch Me

Here are the answers to the lyrics questions.

A41. "Halo" starts with the lyrics, "Remember those walls I built, well baby they're tumbling down." The song describes the feeling of finding a new and overwhelming love.

A42. "Resentment" starts with the lyrics, "You're everything I thought you never were, and nothing like I thought you could've been." The song expresses feelings of betrayal and heartbreak.

A43. "Rocket" starts with the lyrics, "I love your face, you love the taste." The song is known for its sensual and intimate lyrics.

A44. "Broken-Hearted Girl" starts with the lyrics, "I thought that things like this get better with time." The song deals with the pain and confusion of a troubled relationship.

A45. "Sorry" starts with the lyrics, "Ten Hail Marys, I meditate for practice." The song is an unapologetic anthem of independence and self-respect.

A46. "Flawless" starts with the lyrics, "I been on, I been on, I been on." The song is a declaration of confidence and empowerment.

A47. "Upgrade U" starts with the lyrics, "Baby I see you working hard, I want to let you know I'm proud." The song celebrates the partnership and mutual support in a relationship.

A48. "6 Inch" starts with the lyrics, "I've been waking up drenched in sweat." The song features The Weeknd and discusses the hustle and grind.

A49. "Love Drought" starts with the lyrics, "I tried to change, closed my mouth more." This song explores themes of reconciliation and healing in a relationship.

A50. "All Night" starts with the lyrics, "I remember being young, so brave I knew what I needed." This song celebrates enduring love and forgiveness.

Halfway through already! Now let's have some album-related questions.

Q51. Which album features the song "Crazy in Love"?
    A. 4
    B. B'Day
    C. Dangerously in Love
    D. I Am... Sasha Fierce

Q52. Which album features the song "Irreplaceable"?
    A. 4
    B. B'Day
    C. Dangerously in Love
    D. I Am... Sasha Fierce

Q53. Which album features the song "Single Ladies (Put a Ring on It)"?
    A. 4
    B. B'Day
    C. Dangerously in Love
    D. I Am... Sasha Fierce

Q54. Which album features the song "Halo"?
    A. 4
    B. B'Day
    C. Dangerously in Love
    D. I Am... Sasha Fierce

Q55. Which album features the song "Love on Top"?

A. 4
B. B'Day
C. Dangerously in Love
D. I Am... Sasha Fierce

Q56. Which album features the song "Drunk in Love"?
   A. 4
   B. Beyoncé
   C. Dangerously in Love
   D. Lemonade

Q57. Which album features the song "Formation"?
   A. 4
   B. Beyoncé
   C. Dangerously in Love
   D. Lemonade

Q58. Which album features the song "Partition"?
   A. 4
   B. Beyoncé
   C. Dangerously in Love
   D. Lemonade

Q59. Which album features the song "Run the World (Girls)"?
   A. 4
   B. B'Day
   C. Dangerously in Love
   D. I Am... Sasha Fierce

Q60. Which album features the song "XO"?
   A. 4
   B. Beyoncé
   C. Dangerously in Love
   D. Lemonade

Here are the answers to the album-related questions.

A51. The song "Crazy in Love" is featured on the album "Dangerously in Love." This debut solo album solidified Beyoncé's status as a major solo artist and includes collaborations with Jay-Z.

A52. The song "Irreplaceable" is featured on the album "B'Day." This album showcases Beyoncé's versatility and includes several chart-topping hits.

A53. The song "Single Ladies (Put a Ring on It)" is featured on the album "I Am... Sasha Fierce." The song's iconic dance routine and empowering message made it a global sensation.

A54. The song "Halo" is featured on the album "I Am... Sasha Fierce." This album highlights Beyoncé's vocal range and includes a mix of powerful ballads and upbeat tracks.

A55. The song "Love on Top" is featured on the album "4." This album marked a shift in Beyoncé's musical style and includes a variety of genres and influences.

A56. The song "Drunk in Love" is featured on the self-titled album "Beyoncé." The album was released as a surprise and is known for its experimental sound and visual album format.

A57. The song "Formation" is featured on the album "Lemonade." This album addresses themes of infidelity, empowerment, and resilience and includes a visual component.

A58. The song "Partition" is featured on the self-titled album "Beyoncé." The song's provocative lyrics and visuals highlight Beyoncé's bold and confident persona.

A59. The song "Run the World (Girls)" is featured on the album "4." This feminist anthem celebrates female empowerment and has become one of Beyoncé's signature songs.

A60. The song "XO" is featured on the self-titled album "Beyoncé." The song is a love letter to her fans and showcases a more vulnerable and intimate side of Beyoncé.

Here is the next set of questions.

Q61. Who was the producer of Beyoncé's "Dangerously in Love" album?
    A. Darkchild
    B. Kanye West
    C. Scott Storch
    D. Timbaland

Q62. Who was the producer of Beyoncé's "Lemonade" album?
    A. Diplo
    B. Just Blaze
    C. Pharrell Williams
    D. Timbaland

Q63. Who did Beyoncé collaborate with on the song "Beautiful Liar"?
    A. Alicia Keys
    B. Lady Gaga
    C. Shakira
    D. Rihanna

Q64. Who performed the duet "Deja Vu" with Beyoncé?
    A. Chris Brown
    B. Drake
    C. Jay-Z
    D. Kanye West

Q65. Who featured with Beyoncé on the song "Love in This Club Part II"?
   A. Justin Timberlake
   B. Ludacris
   C. Ne-Yo
   D. Usher

Q66. Who did Beyoncé duet with on the song "Put It in a Love Song"?
   A. Alicia Keys
   B. Kelly Rowland
   C. Mary J. Blige
   D. Rihanna

Q67. Who joined Beyoncé on the song "Until the End of Time"?
   A. Bruno Mars
   B. Justin Timberlake
   C. Pharrell Williams
   D. Robin Thicke

Q68. Who collaborated with Beyoncé on the song "Walk on Water"?
   A. Drake
   B. Eminem
   C. Jay-Z
   D. Kanye West

Q69. Who performed "Hymn for the Weekend" with Beyoncé?

A. Coldplay
B. Maroon 5
C. OneRepublic
D. U2

Q70. Who did Beyoncé team up with for the song "Beautiful Nightmare"?
A. Bruno Mars
B. Jay-Z
C. Ne-Yo
D. The-Dream

Hope you're having fun. Here is the latest set of answers.

A61. Scott Storch was one of the key producers of Beyoncé's "Dangerously in Love" album. His work on this album contributed to its diverse sound and immense success, including hits like "Naughty Girl."

A62. Diplo was one of the prominent producers on Beyoncé's "Lemonade" album. His eclectic production style helped shape the album's innovative and genre-blending sound.

A63. Beyoncé collaborated with Shakira on the song "Beautiful Liar" in 2007. This duet showcases the chemistry and vocal harmonies between the two international superstars.

A64. Beyoncé performed the duet "Deja Vu" with Jay-Z. This energetic track was a hit in 2006 and highlights the dynamic partnership between Beyoncé and Jay-Z.

A65. Usher featured with Beyoncé on the song "Love in This Club Part II." This remix adds Beyoncé's powerful vocals to Usher's original hit.

A66. Beyoncé dueted with Alicia Keys on the song "Put It in a Love Song." The collaboration between these two powerhouse singers was released in 2010.

A67. Justin Timberlake joined Beyoncé on the song "Until the End of Time." This duet is a remix of Timberlake's original track and was released in 2007.

A68. Eminem collaborated with Beyoncé on the song "Walk on Water." This introspective track was released in 2017 and features Beyoncé's emotive vocals.

A69. Coldplay performed "Hymn for the Weekend" with Beyoncé. The song, released in 2015, combines Coldplay's distinctive sound with Beyoncé's powerful voice.

A70. The-Dream teamed up with Beyoncé for the song "Beautiful Nightmare," also known as "Sweet Dreams." This collaboration resulted in a memorable hit with hauntingly beautiful melodies.

Here is the next set of questions:

Q71. In which year did Beyoncé perform at the Super Bowl halftime show for the first time?
  A. 2010
  B. 2012
  C. 2014
  D. 2016

Q72. What is the name of Beyoncé's alter ego, which she introduced in her third studio album?
  A. Queen B
  B. Sasha Fierce
  C. Yoncé
  D. Honey B

Q73. What fragrance did Beyoncé release in 2010?
  A. Heat
  B. Pulse
  C. Rise
  D. Temptation

Q74. Which film did Beyoncé star in alongside Jennifer Hudson and Eddie Murphy?
  A. Austin Powers in Goldmember
  B. Cadillac Records
  C. Dreamgirls
  D. Obsessed

Q75. Which Beyoncé album is often referred to as a visual album due to its extensive use of accompanying videos?
   A. 4
   B. Beyoncé
   C. Lemonade
   D. The Lion King: The Gift

Q76. Beyoncé voiced which character in the 2019 remake of "The Lion King"?
   A. Nala
   B. Sarabi
   C. Shenzi
   D. Zazu

Q77. What is the name of Beyoncé's autobiographical documentary released in 2013?
   A. Beyoncé: Life is But a Dream
   B. Beyoncé: Year of 4
   C. Homecoming: A Film by Beyoncé
   D. Lemonade

Q78. What is the name of the charity organization founded by Beyoncé?
   A. BEYGOOD
   B. Destiny's Foundation
   C. Halo Foundation
   D. Sasha's Dream

Q79. Which animated film features Beyoncé voicing the character Queen Tara?

A. Epic
B. Frozen
C. Moana
D. Zootopia

Q80. What business venture did Beyoncé launch with her mother?

A. A fashion line
B. A music label
C. A perfume brand
D. A production company

Here are the answers to the latest questions.

A71. Beyoncé first performed at the Super Bowl halftime show in 2013. Her performance was widely praised and included a reunion with her Destiny's Child bandmates.

A72. Beyoncé's alter ego introduced in her third studio album is "Sasha Fierce." This persona was used to express her more aggressive and sensual side in her music and performances.

A73. Beyoncé released her fragrance "Beyoncé Heat" in 2010. The scent became a best-seller, showcasing her influence beyond music and into the world of fashion and beauty.

A74. Beyoncé starred in "Dreamgirls" alongside Jennifer Hudson and Eddie Murphy. Released in 2006, the film earned critical acclaim, and Beyoncé's performance as Deena Jones was particularly noted.

A75. The album "Beyoncé," released in 2013, is often referred to as a visual album. It included a music video for every song, breaking traditional album release norms and showcasing her innovative approach to music and visual arts.

A76. Beyoncé voiced the character Nala in the 2019 remake of "The Lion King." Her performance brought a new dimension to the character and added star power to the film's voice cast.

A77. Beyoncé's autobiographical documentary released in 2013 is titled "Beyoncé: Life is But a Dream." The documentary gives an intimate look at her life and career, featuring personal footage and interviews.

A78. The charity organization founded by Beyoncé is named "BEYGOOD." It aims to support various humanitarian causes, including disaster relief, education, and women's empowerment.

A79. Beyoncé voices the character Queen Tara in the animated film "Epic." Released in 2013, the film features her as the elegant and powerful queen of the forest.

A80. Beyoncé launched a fashion line called House of Deréon with her mother Tina. This venture combines their fashion sensibilities and offers stylish clothing for women.

Let's have some more lyrics related questions.

Q81. Which song contains the lyrics, "I'm a survivor, I'm not gonna give up"?
    A. Halo
    B. Irreplaceable
    C. Run the World (Girls)
    D. Survivor

Q82. Which song contains the lyrics, "To the left, to the left, everything you own in the box to the left"?
    A. Crazy in Love
    B. Halo
    C. Irreplaceable
    D. Single Ladies (Put a Ring on It)

Q83. Which song contains the lyrics, "Baby, it's you, you're the one I love, you're the one I need"?
    A. Crazy in Love
    B. Love on Top
    C. Partition
    D. XO

Q84. Which song contains the lyrics, "We be all night, love, love"?
    A. Crazy in Love
    B. Drunk in Love
    C. Halo
    D. Partition

Q85. Which song contains the lyrics, "I took a vow that from now on, I'm gonna be my own best friend"?
   A. Crazy in Love
   B. Me, Myself and I
   C. Single Ladies (Put a Ring on It)
   D. Sorry

Q86. Which song contains the lyrics, "I wake up looking this good and I wouldn't change it if I could"?
   A. Flawless
   B. Formation
   C. Partition
   D. Pretty Hurts

Q87. Which song contains the lyrics, "Boy, you're looking like you like what you see"?
   A. Baby Boy
   B. Check on It
   C. Déjà Vu
   D. Naughty Girl

Q88. Which song contains the lyrics, "Let me sit this ass on you"?
   A. Drunk in Love
   B. Haunted
   C. Rocket
   D. XO

Q89. Which song contains the lyrics, "Your love is bright as ever, even in the shadows"?
- A. Halo
- B. Mine
- C. Partition
- D. XO

Q90. Which song contains the lyrics, "So go ahead and get gone, call up that chick and see if she's home"?
- A. Best Thing I Never Had
- B. Irreplaceable
- C. Me, Myself and I
- D. Sorry

Here are the answers to the last set of questions.

A81. The lyrics "I'm a survivor, I'm not gonna give up" are from "Survivor." This empowering anthem was performed by Destiny's Child and celebrates resilience and strength.

A82. The lyrics "To the left, to the left, everything you own in the box to the left" are from "Irreplaceable." This song's theme of independence and moving on from a bad relationship resonated with many listeners.

A83. The lyrics "Baby, it's you, you're the one I love, you're the one I need" are from "Love on Top." This upbeat song celebrates love and commitment and is notable for its key changes.

A84. The lyrics "We be all night, love, love" are from "Drunk in Love." This sultry track features Jay-Z and highlights the passionate and playful side of their relationship.

A85. The lyrics "I took a vow that from now on, I'm gonna be my own best friend" are from "Me, Myself and I." This song focuses on self-love and independence after a breakup.

A86. The lyrics "I wake up looking this good and I wouldn't change it if I could" are from "Flawless."

This track promotes self-confidence and features a famous speech by Chimamanda Ngozi Adichie.

A87. The lyrics "Boy, you're looking like you like what you see" are from "Naughty Girl." The song has a seductive vibe and showcases Beyoncé's flirtatious side.

A88. The lyrics "Let me sit this ass on you" are from "Rocket." This song is known for its sensual and intimate lyrics and was inspired by D'Angelo's "Untitled (How Does It Feel)."

A89. The lyrics "Your love is bright as ever, even in the shadows" are from "XO." This song celebrates love and the joy it brings, with an anthemic chorus.

A90. The lyrics "So go ahead and get gone, call up that chick and see if she's home" are from "Irreplaceable." This song's theme of independence and empowerment has made it one of Beyoncé's most memorable hits.

Here goes with the final set of questions.

Q91. How many Grammy Awards has Beyoncé won?
   A. 22
   B. 24
   C. 26
   D. 28

Q92. When did Beyoncé win her first Grammy award?
   A. 2000
   B. 2001
   C. 2002
   D. 2003

Q93. Which album earned Beyoncé the Grammy Award for Album of the Year?
   A. 4
   B. Beyoncé
   C. Dangerously in Love
   D. Lemonade

Q94. Which album earned Beyoncé the Grammy Award for Best Urban Contemporary Album in 2017?
   A. 4
   B. Beyoncé
   C. Dangerously in Love
   D. Lemonade

Q95. Which award did Beyoncé win at the 2021 Grammy Awards?
   A. Best New Artist
   B. Best Pop Vocal Album
   C. Best R&B Performance
   D. Best Rap Performance

Q96. Which award show honored Beyoncé with the Icon Award in 2020?
   A. American Music Awards
   B. BET Awards
   C. Billboard Music Awards
   D. MTV Video Music Awards

Q97. What is Beyoncé's official website address?
   A. beyonce.com
   B. beyonceofficial.com
   C. queenbey.com
   D. thebeyhive.com

Q98. What is Beyoncé's official Instagram account?
   A. @beyonce
   B. @beyonceofficial
   C. @queenbey
   D. @thebeyonce

Q99. What is Beyoncé's official X (formerly known as Twitter) account?
   A. @beyonce
   B. @beyonceofficial

C. @queenbeyonce
D. @thebeyhive

Q100. What is Beyoncé's best-selling single of all time?
A. Crazy in Love
B. Halo
C. Irreplaceable
D. Single Ladies (Put a Ring on It)

Q101. What are Beyoncé's fans called?
A. Beyhive
B. Beysquad
C. Queen's Court
D. The Beystans

Here is the final set of answers.

A91. At the end of 2024, Beyoncé has won 28 Grammy Awards. This impressive number makes her one of the most awarded artists in Grammy history, showcasing her incredible talent and influence in the music industry.

A92. Beyoncé won her first Grammy award in 2001 as a member of Destiny's Child. The group received the award for Best R&B Performance by a Duo or Group with Vocals for the song "Say My Name."

A93. "Lemonade" earned Beyoncé the Grammy Award for Best Urban Contemporary Album. "Lemonade" was critically acclaimed for its bold themes and innovative production.

A94. "Lemonade" earned Beyoncé the Grammy Award for Best Urban Contemporary Album in 2017. The album was critically acclaimed for its bold themes and innovative production.

A95. Beyoncé won the Best R&B Performance award at the 2021 Grammy Awards for her song "Black Parade." This song, celebrating Black culture and activism, was released on Juneteenth in 2020.

A96. Beyoncé was honored with the Icon Award at the 2020 BET Awards. This award recognized her outstanding contributions to music, culture, and philanthropy.

A97. Beyoncé's official website address is beyonce.com. This site features the latest news, tour dates, music releases, and exclusive content related to Beyoncé.

A98. Beyoncé's official Instagram account is @beyonce. Her Instagram account is known for its artistic photos, personal moments, and updates on her projects.

A99. Beyoncé's official X (formerly Twitter) account is @beyonce. She uses this platform to share updates, announcements, and engage with her fans.

A100. Beyoncé's best-selling single of all time is "Single Ladies (Put a Ring on It)." The song's catchy beat, empowering lyrics, and iconic dance moves have made it a timeless hit.

A101. Beyoncé's fans are called the Beyhive. This dedicated fanbase is known for their unwavering support and enthusiasm for Beyoncé's music and projects.

That's a great question to finish with.

I hope you enjoyed this book, and I hope you got most of the answers right. I also hope you learnt some new things about the legend Beyoncé!

If you have any comments or if you see anything wrong, please email support@glowwormpress.com and we'll get the book updated. We have updated the book thanks to other Beyoncé fans, and we do read every email.

If this book was a gift, there is just one thing left to do and that's to ask the person who got this book for you to leave a positive review on Amazon saying what you think of Beyoncé.

We have been told her team loves reading reviews.

Many thanks in advance.

Printed in Dunstable, United Kingdom

73247469R00037